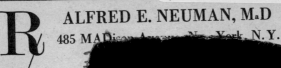

R ALFRED E. NEUMAN, M.D
485 MADison Avenue, New York, N.Y.

For MADicinal Purposes Only

For UPSET
attributed to the World Situation . . .
    Play "MODERN CHESS"
        at every new depressing development!

For NAUSEA
brought on by seeing Modern Movies . . .
    Read "HOLLYWOOD SURPLUS SALE"
        after every disgusting double feature!

For DISTRESS
cause by Modern Merchandising . . .
    Try "DISCOUNT CENTER OWNER OF THE YEAR"
        before your next shopping trip!

For GAS
generated by our Biased Newspapers . . .
    Swallow "THE DAILY MONOPLOY"
        every morning and*or evening!

For any other COMPLAINS OR SYMPTOMS . .
    take . . .
            "THE INDIGESTIBLE MAD"
            FOR INSTANT RELIEF!

                                    A.E.N.
                                    MaD

William M. Gaines's

THE INDIGESTIBLE

Albert B. Feldstein, Editor

A SIGNET BOOK from

NEW AMERICAN LIBRARY

TIMES MIRROR

SIGNET TRADEMARK REG. U.S. PAT. OFF. AND FOREIGN COUNTRIES
REGISTERED TRADEMARK—MARCA REGISTRADA
HECHO EN CHICAGO, U.S.A.

SIGNET, SIGNET CLASSICS, SIGNETTE, MENTOR AND PLUME BOOKS
are published *in the United States* by
The New American Library, Inc.,
1301 Avenue of the Americas, New York, New York 10019,
in Canada by The New American Library of Canada Limited,
81 Mack Avenue, Scarborough, 704, Ontario,
in the United Kingdom by The New English Library Limited,
Barnard's Inn, Holborn, London, E.C. 1, England

FIRST PRINTING, MARCH, 1968

PRINTED IN THE UNITED STATES OF AMERICA

THE INDIGESTIBLE

MAD

When Don Martin is mixing the drinks, you can rest assured that the results will be "Bottoms Up!" . . . especially when he tries to duplicate the experiments of his idols:

DR. JEKYLL
AND
MR. HYDE

6

LIGHTS, CAMERA, AUCTION DEPT.

Recently, we read that the M-G-M studios, in order to recoup some of the huge expenses incurred by Marlon Brando while making "Mutiny on the Bounty," has offered to sell the "Bounty"—which was constructed especially for

HOLLY
SURPLUS

ARTIST: GEORGE WOODBRIDGE   WRITER: EARLE DOUD

the movie. Maybe they should have offered to sell Marlon Brando instead. Anyway, the idea of selling old movie props to offset the modern production costs could catch on—and then we'd be seeing ads like these in our newspapers, announcing another

WOOD SALE

PET LOVERS!
2,152 SPECIALLY-TRAINED
CATS

These cats were specially-trained to knock over garbage can lids, ash trays, etc.,—then freeze in the searchlight beam—at the sound of approaching low voices speaking in German or Japanese.

ONLY $10 EACH

CLOSE CALL WAR PROPS, INC., Hollywood, Calif.

13

GUNS! GUNS! GUNS!

NOW YOU CAN OWN ONE OR MORE OF THESE UNIQUE MOVIE GUNS!

HERO'S GUN

Shoots only hands. Even when pointed at head, neck or stomach and fired — will still hit only the hand.

VILLAIN'S GUN

Cannot kill anybody! Just point it at person two feet away — it will miss!

DETECTIVE'S GUN

Absolutely harmless. Only shoots locks and knobs off doors.

INDIAN WAR HERO RIFLE

Absolutely fabulous. Each bullet kills five Indians at same time.

EARLY PIONEER WOMAN'S RIFLE

When pointed up in the air and fired with eyes closed, will kill Indian on fast horse 500 yds. away

GUNS OF NAVARONE

Only two available! Perfect for person who now owns two 400-ft. holsters!

CLICK GUN

Made of rubber. Will not fire. Just clicks 3 times — then is used to throw at hero. Will not injure.

KICK GUN

Will not fire. Flat on one side. Perfect for kicking back and forth across floor during fights!

ONLY $18.00 EACH

EXTRA BONUS! With each order, we'll send absolutely free a genuine Police Dept. Gun. Not a Hollywood fabrication, but an actual gun like the one used by most city Police Departments. Only shoots innocent bystanders.

Murderous Props, Inc. Hollywood, California

20

CLOCKS! CLOCKS! CLOCKS!

TREMENDOUS ASSORTMENT

ALL MAKES AND
MODELS—FROM
"GRANDFATHER"
TO "ALARM"

ONLY
$5.95
EACH

Handsome — Decorative! Used in hundreds of movies to denote the passage of time. Only one drawback. They're not terribly accurate. In fact, the hands spin around at a fantastic speed, registering 24 hours in 10 seconds.

DAYS LATER PROPS, INC. HOLLYWOOD, CALIFORNIA

"Why Did The Chicken Cross The Road?" is a riddle that has been plaguing mankind for thousands of years — or however long it's been since chickens started crossing roads. Today's comic strip cartoonists, with their individual approaches, might help us find a new solution to this problem — or confuse it even more. Anyway, here is MAD's idea of what might appear in your daily papers

IF FIVE COMIC STRIP CARTOONISTS INTERPRETED THE AGE-OLD RIDDLE:

"WHY DID THE CHICKEN CROSS THE ROAD?"

ARTIST: WALLACE WOOD
WRITER: GARY BELKIN

MARK TRAIL   by Ed Dodd

PEANUTS   by Charles M. Schulz

LOOK AT ME! LOOK AT WHAT I'M **DOING!** I'M CROSSING THE ROAD AGAIN! THIS IS THE **FOURTH** TIME THIS WEEK THAT I'VE CROSSED THE ROAD!

WHY? -- I ASK MYSELF! WHY DO I **CROSS** THE ROAD? WHAT IS THE DEEPER PSYCHOLOGICAL MOTIVATION INHERENT IN THIS SIMPLE ACT?

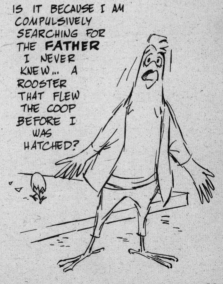

PERHAPS SOME DAY I WILL CROSS THE ROAD FOR THE LAST TIME. PERHAPS THEN MY PROBLEMS WILL ALL BE SOLVED, AND I WILL FIND **TRUE HAPPINESS** IN THOSE LAST BRIEF MOMENTS BEFORE I AM SUMMONED TO THAT GREAT DEEP-FAT FRYER IN THE SKY!

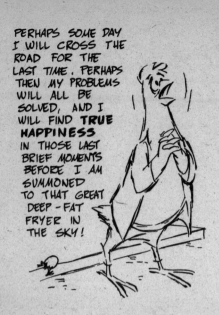

MEANWHILE, I WILL **KEEP ON** CROSSING THE ROAD ... MAINLY BECAUSE MY **PSYCHIATRIST** LIVES ON THE OTHER SIDE!!

MISS PEACH — by Mel Lazarus

CORN POEM DEPT.

Following are some new versions of popular old poems. Well, so much for the introduction. Er — come to think of it, maybe we'd better pad the introduction. The MAD reader, being a creature of habit, expects long introductions. The MAD reader, also being a lazy slob, never reads the introductions. So, since it doesn't really matter what we put here, this is as good a time as any to list Jack Armstrong's 3 important training rules: First, make a friend of soap and water because dirt breeds germs and germs can make people sickly and weak. Second, get plenty of fresh air, sleep, and exercise. And third, every morning, eat a heaping bowl of Wheaties with plenty of milk, cream, sugar, and your favorite fruit. Oh, we almost forgot. We call this article

A CHILD'S GARDEN OF WEEDS

ARTIST: JOE ORLANDO   WRITER: LARRY SIEGEL

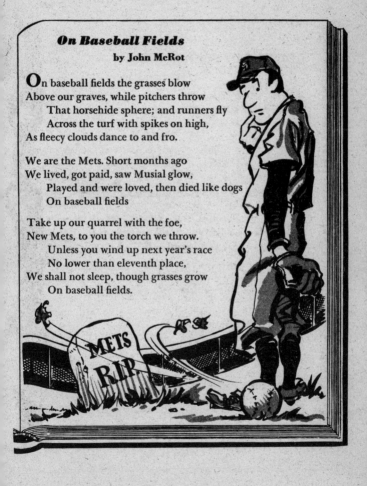

On Baseball Fields
by John McRot

On baseball fields the grasses blow
Above our graves, while pitchers throw
    That horsehide sphere; and runners fly
    Across the turf with spikes on high,
As fleecy clouds dance to and fro.

We are the Mets. Short months ago
We lived, got paid, saw Musial glow,
    Played and were loved, then died like dogs
    On baseball fields

Take up our quarrel with the foe,
New Mets, to you the torch we throw.
    Unless you wind up next year's race
    No lower than eleventh place,
We shall not sleep, though grasses grow
    On baseball fields.

METS
R.I.P.

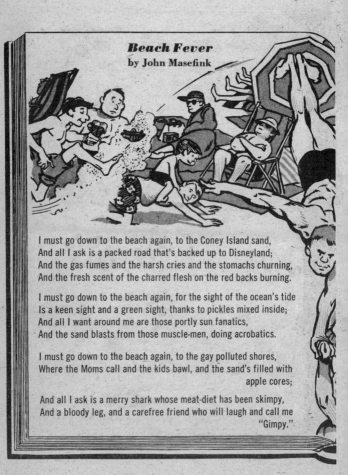

Beach Fever
by John Masefink

I must go down to the beach again, to the Coney Island sand,
And all I ask is a packed road that's backed up to Disneyland;
And the gas fumes and the harsh cries and the stomachs churning,
And the fresh scent of the charred flesh on the red backs burning.

I must go down to the beach again, for the sight of the ocean's tide
Is a keen sight and a green sight, thanks to pickles mixed inside;
And all I want around me are those portly sun fanatics,
And the sand blasts from those muscle-men, doing acrobatics.

I must go down to the beach again, to the gay polluted shores,
Where the Moms call and the kids bawl, and the sand's filled with
                                                    apple cores;

And all I ask is a merry shark whose meat-diet has been skimpy,
And a bloody leg, and a carefree friend who will laugh and call me
                                                    "Gimpy."

38

I Remember
by Thomas Hoot

I remember, I remember,
    The house where I was born,
The little bathroom down the hall
    Where 19 raced each morn.
My 13 brothers hated me,
    My sisters felt the same.
Mom never called me up to eat;
    She didn't know my name.

I remember, I remember,
    The walls so pale and white
That turned a vivid bloody red
    When Mum and Dad would fight.
I learned about the birds and bees
    When I was ten and three.
But I was so confused I thought
    That I should wed a bee.

I remember, I remember,
    The joys my schoolhouse gave,
How I came late for second grade
    Because I had to shave.
I think that I shall ne'er forget
    A girl named Emmy Lou.
I carried home her books from school
    (Her boy friend told me to).

I remember, I remember,
    All kinds of boyhood things.
How glad I am these memories
    Can launch my heart on wings.
They bring much pleasure to my life
    And give me quite a kick.
They also help my analyst
    To find out why I'm sick.

Courage

by Robert W. Tsouris

When you're lost in the wood, and things don't look too good,
　　And defeat is smack in your sight,
When you're scared as all hell, a voice in you may yell,
　　"Get right in there, fellow, and fight!"
Perseverance persists, so you knot up your fists,
　　To battle with life, come what may;
But you might just get hurt rollin' there in the dirt . . .
　　Have you thought about runnin' away?

When you find life a chore, and the wolf's at your door,
　　And you're faced with a terrible plight,
And your back's to the wall and your chances are small . . .
　　Run off like a thief in the night!
Just learn how to quit and you'll never get hit,
　　And your eyes won't be moistened by tears.
Heroes' songs may be sung, but those suckers die young . . .
　　While you—you'll live ninety-eight years!

The Hunter's Hour
by Henry W. Lungfellow

Between the dawn and the sunset,
  When the day is a-bloom like a flower,
Comes a pause in card-playing and drinking
  That is known as the Hunter's Hour.

We hear in the woods there before us
  An ominous forest beat,
The sound of Nature erupting,
  The rumble of animals' feet.

From our tent flaps we see in the sunlight,
  While sipping our golden Schlitz beers,
A chipmunk, a man-eating squirrel,
  And a bunny with floppy ears.

A whisper, and then a silence:
  Yet they know by our merry eyes
We are plotting and planning together
  To blast them down like flies.

A sudden dash for machine guns,
  A sudden rush for grenades!
A pause while our rifles are fixed with
  The bayonets' shiny blades.

Then into the forest we scamper,
  Our firearms blazing their flames,
We jolly good fellows and sportsmen
  Engaged in our glorious games.

Do you think, O foolish law-makers
   Who are fighting to see our sport fall,
That the nation's noble gun lobbies
   Are not a match for you all?

We'll all go on hunting forever,
   Yes, forever we'll blast away—
Till the forests resemble North Clark Street
   In Chicago, that Valentine's Day.

Young Fellow My Son
by Robert W. Servecorn

"**W**here are you going, young fellow my son
    On this beautiful day in May?"
"I'm going to find me a wife now, Mom;
    There are women around, they say!"
"But you're only a child, young fellow my son!
    You aren't obliged to wed!"
"I'm forty-five-and-a-half now, Mom!
    Who knows, I may soon be dead!"

"So you're off to wed, young fellow my son,
    To desert your mother, you mean?"
"I'm terribly sorry to leave you, Mom,
    But I've been home since June '17!"
"You're breaking my heart, young fellow my son,
    You're causing your mother torment."
"I'm forty-five-and-a-half now, Mom;
    I'm as old as the President!"

"Why don't you call, young fellow my son?
    I sit by the phone and pray.
I miss you so, and I'm awfully glum,
    It's an hour since you've gone away.
And I've had the fire in the parlor lit,
    And I'm holding your teddy bear tight!
Till my baby comes home, here I will sit
    Into the quiet night."

"You're home, you're home, young fellow my son!
    You've changed! Do you feel all right?
I haven't seen you since 7:01;
    Why didn't you call or write?"
"I've found me a beautiful woman, Mom,
    And would like to make her my wife!"
"My heart! I'm dying, young fellow my son!
    My baby is ending my life!"

"Where are you going, young fellow my son
    On this beautiful day in May?"
"I'd still like to find me a wife, dear Mom;
    There are girls yet around, they say!"
"But you're only a child, young fellow my son!
    You're causing your mother torment!"
"I'm sixty-eight! But forget it, Mom—
    Er—have you seen my Polident?"

The Village Druggist

by Henry Wadsworth Longswallow

Under the towering Rx sign
    The village druggist stands.
Oh what a mighty man is he,
    Unbowed by his job's demands.
Yes, many's the ham and rye I've had
    Made by his sinewy hands.

His hair is long and coarse and grey,
    His face is etched with pain.
His eyes are dark, but kindly yet,
    Though crises fog his brain:
Shall he re-stock "The Tropic of Cancer'
    Or switch to Mickey Spillane?

Week in, week out, from morn till night
    With his tools of trade he camps.
A modern Grecian god is he
    There 'neath fluorescent lamps,
As he looks the whole world in the face
    And tears off postage stamps.

When the pains of life weigh on his bro
    And he's filled with misery,
I take my druggist by the hand
    (The one more sinewy)
And he finds some Bromo and Bufferin
    Down at the A&P.

It Cannot Be Done
by Edgar A. Gassed

A fellow once said it cannot be done,
  But I gave a laugh and cried out
That "maybe it's true, but I would be one
  To give it a good healthy bout!"
So I spit on my palms, rolled my sleeves up my arms,
  In a second or two I'd begun it.
I started to sing as I tackled the thing
  That cannot be done, AND I DONE IT!

(So what did you expect, the obvious trick ending where the
  guy *wouldn't* be able to do it? Besides, since this is an
  Edgar A. Gassed poem, it's just as funny, straight!)

The author of the following article has agreed to take full responsibility for it . . . mainly because the rest of us are "chicken", and we'd like to stay on the good side of our wives, girl friends and other members of the opposite sex who might not see anything funny about . . .

THE LIGHTER SIDE OF

Women

WRITER & ARTIST: DAVID BERG

Who was at the door?

You'll never believe it! It was a door-to-door **brush salesman!** And he handed me the corniest old line. You know that old routine: "Is your **mother** in, young lady?"

Then he gives me that phony business of how I look like **a teenager**—and how I could **never** be the mother of a nine-year-old child—and how you must've robbed the **cradle** when you married me! You know, that asinine old **baloney!**

Really? I thought that kind of sales pitch went out with the bustle!

It did . . .

. . . BUT I'M AFRAID IT STILL WORKS!!

51

Doctor, I can't **stand** it! I've got this **terrible toothache!!**

Please! **Please!** Can you give me an **appointment** for today??

Okay! If you come down right now, I'll squeeze you in!

N-now? Oh, no! I **couldn't** do that! I've got an appointment at the **Hairdresser** in fifteen minutes!

54

56

59

62

Have you ever waited for a reply to a letter . . . and finally, with your patience exhausted, fired off a hasty follow-up letter . . . only to return home after mailing it to find the answer to your original letter? Of course not! Because you're reading MAD, which means you're illiterate in the first place! But if it ever did happen to you, you may get a kick out of this next article which is concerned with

Letters That Cross In The Mail

ARTIST: BOB CLARKE

WRITER: DICK DE BARTOLO

You're reading the newspaper, and you see a stock offer: "Missile Electronics Corp., $1.00 a share, Dividends to be guaranteed after one year . . ." You always wanted to play the big business tycoon, so you buy 100 shares. You wait the year—no dividends—nothing. You wait one month longer—still nothing. So you fire off this hot missive:

Missile Electronics, Corp.
Bently Salt Flats
Ogden, Utah
   To whom it may concern:
You can fool some of the people
some of the time, but you can't
fool me! I now realize that
your so-called stock is a phony,
and I want my $100. back.
I better get it, too, or I'll report
you to the SEC and the Better
Business Bureau. The worthless
stock certificates, which I have
signed over, are enclosed. I never
want to see them again. Maybe
you can sell them to some new sucker!
                    Signed,
                    Nobody's Fool

That night, when you get home from work, this is waiting:

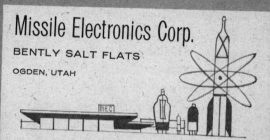

Missile Electronics Corp.

BENTLY SALT FLATS

OGDEN, UTAH

Dear Stockholder:

Your patience has been rewarded.

You've undoubtedly been reading about the merger in the newspapers, but this notice makes it official.

MISSILE ELECTRONICS will merge with E.I. DU PONT & CO., INC., effective in 15 days.

MISSILE ELECTRONICS stockholders will receive one share of DU PONT stock for each share of MISSILE ELECTRONIC stock they now own.

In other words, those $1.00 Stock Certificates you now hold will be worth about $185.00 each!

Congratulations on a shrewd investment, and don't let those Stock Certificates out of your sight!

Sincerely,

Irving I. Missile

Irving I. Missile
President

You rent an apartment, but there's never enough heat or hot water, and the fuses are forever blowing. You write notes to your landlord asking that something be done, but there's never any satisfaction. So you start looking, and you finally find the apartment of your dreams. Now's your chance to really tell that landlord what you think of him! With your last rent check, you enclose a little note . . .

Dear Mr. Rhinehart,

Guess what, you old bloodsucker! I finally wised up, and I'm moving from this flea-bitten, cruddy, run-down flop house you laughingly call an apartment building. I managed to tolerate it long enough to find a place worthy of living in, and come the first of next month, I'll be leaving this dump — if it doesn't collapse before then!

Thank God my lease is up. I couldn't have lasted here much longer. And never having to see your ugly face again makes moving out all the more pleasant!

a former cell-mate,

E. Lawrence

You take the letter to the Post Office — (You can't wait for a regular pick-up at the corner mail box!) — and off it goes. But when you return home, there's a letter under your door. It's from the landlord of your *new* apartment!

IDEAL TERRACE APARTMENTS

"Overlooking The Park"

A. Glink, Manager

Dear Mr. Lawrence :-

It was most pleasant talking with you yesterday. Unfortunately, since I spoke with you, a little problem has arisen.

Both I <u>and</u> my wife accidentally rented the same apartment to two different people. And since it is the only apartment available, we must now decide which party to give it to.

In order to make a fair decision, we have written to your present landlord to ask him his opinion of you as a tenant.

The apartment is nearly yours. All we have to do now is to hear from your landlord.

Sincerely,

Arnold Glink

Arnold Glink

You apply for a job, and the Personnel Director tells you he'll notify you of the firm's decision by the end of the week. So you wait—and nothing. You wait two weeks—still nothing. You're so mad, you write the Personnel Director:

Dear Mr. Clayton,

Well, Chum—the week I was supposed to wait is up, and so is the following week, and you didn't have the common decency to write me—even if it was to tell me I wasn't the right man for the job.

That's why I'm writing to you...to thank you for NOT hiring me!! Any company that has such little consideration for the feelings of others must be a rotten outfit to do business with. I probably would have been miserable working for such a two-bit firm anyway, so I consider myself lucky. As for my asking $150. a week salary---I just pulled that ridiculous figure out of my hat!

Give my deepest sympathy to whoever gets stuck with the job!

Still happy—
Arthur Mushbarker

You mail the letter, happy that you've given vent to your pent-up anger. But when you return home after another day of unsuccessful job-hunting, this letter is in your box:

From The Desk Of J. L. CLAYTON
PERSONNEL DIRECTOR
AMERICAN BUNGHOLE MFG. CO.

Dear Mr. Mushbarker:-

Sorry this letter with our decision is so late getting to you, but you accidentally listed your address as 3119 instead of 3191, and it wasn't until the letter was returned and we checked the phone book that we found your correct address.

Now to business...

We feel that you are the man for our firm. I like your honesty. And I was particularly impressed with your desire to start with a small company. As far as salary goes, we will meet your $150 figure.

Our answer is "Yes", Mr. Mushbarker. What is yours?

Sincerely,

J L Clayton

J. L. Clayton

You've entered a contest. The contest closed Nov. 1st and you were supposed to be notified of the winners: It's now January and you've heard nothing so you write the company:

Gentlemen:

I entered your ha-ha-ha contest. It was supposed to be judged after it closed on Nov. 1st... but I never heard anything more about it - and I never even saw a list of the winners. Well, I'd like to say that it's just as well, because I can't stand your cereal anyway. It tastes like wet shredded newspapers -- and I assume that any company which makes a product _that_ _bad_ must advertise phony contests, too!

Disgusted,
Milton Finster

You mail the letter on your way to work, but when you get to your office, your wife telephones. There's an Air Mail letter from the Snappies Cereal Company! She reads it . . .

"SNAPPIES" CEREAL COMPANY
The Best To You Each Evening!
BOTTLE CREEK, VERMONT

Dear Mr. Finster:-

You've undoubtedly been anxious about the results of our contest. Although it was to have closed on Nov. 1st, a printer's error marked a good many "SNAPPIES" boxes: "Contest Closes Jan. 1st." So to keep our contest completely honest, we had to wait the additional time to make our decision. And that brings us to the happy news: Mr. Finster--YOU ARE TIED FOR FIRST PLACE in our contest!

And so, as per our rules, "a 25-word essay on 'I like "SNAPPIES" because...' will be used as a tie-breaker." As you can see, the $25,000.00 First Prize is quite close to being yours. May we have your opinion of our cereal so that we can make our final decision.

We'll be watching for a letter from you!

Sincerely,

Herman L. Snap
President.

Antonio Prohias, who was forced to flee Cuba because he refused to become a "Castro Convertible", brings us another MAD installment of that friendly rivalry between the man in black and the man in white—better known as . . .

GREAT OAFS FROM THE LITTLE ACORNS GROW DEPT.

Every proud parent thinks his kid is a genius, and almost every little thing the brat does is taken as a sure sign of some extraordinary ability or talent that will surely manifest itself in later life. If, however, the little tyke does not fulfill his parents' hopes, it isn't because he failed, but because his parents failed. Mainly, they failed to interpret those early signs correctly! F'rinstance, there are some parents who thought their children would become great artists and writers. You can imagine their shock when their offspring ended up as members of the MAD Magazine staff. With this in mind, here are some other case histories which show . . .

HOW PARENTS GUESS WRONG ABOUT THEIR KIDS' FUTURE CAREERS

ARTIST: BOB CLARKE   WRITER: DON REILLY

THE "PREDICTION"

Our little Herman is destined to do **scientific research!** He loves nothing better than to peer into that toy microscope!

YEARS LATER

THE "PREDICTION"

YEARS LATER

THE "PREDICTION"

Isn't Harvey something . . . the way he always mixes his food! With such an early talent for recipes, he might end up another Oscar of the Waldorf!

YEARS LATER

D.S.C.

THE "PREDICTION"

Have you noticed how Clyde loves to **pour stuff** in and out of old jars and bottles? Betcha it means he's a natural-born **chemist!**

YEARS LATER

THE SUICIDE

PWOING

It's a well-known fact today that more and more newspapers are going out of business, and more and more cities are becoming what are known as "one-newspaper towns." Naturally, the "only newspaper" in a town controls what everyone reads, and can be pretty obnoxious, opinionated, and in-

ALL THE NEWS THAT WE FEEL
LIKE PRINTING, AND IF YOU
DON'T LIKE IT ... TOUGH!

The Daily

"Festerville's **LEADING** Newspaper—bec

FEBRUARY 15, 1963	ARTIST: JOE ORLANDO	WEATHER: There will be no We appearing on TV, and

DAILY MONOPOLY WINS COVETED "HENRY R. LUCE AWARD" FOR EXCELLENCE IN NEWS REPORTING

NEW YORK, Feb. 13 — Henry R. Luce, Editor-in-Chief of LIFE and TIME Magazines, presented *The Daily Monopoly* with his annual award for "Excellent News Reporting" today.

"Of all the newspapers considered," said Luce, "*The Daily Monopoly* most closely follows the long-established journalistic traditions of LIFE and TIME, in not allowing such mundane and unimportant things as facts to stand in the way of the personal feelings and prejudices of its publisher and editor in the presentation of straight news."

Accepting the coveted award for *The Daily Monopoly* at ceremonies held in The Waldorf-Astoria Hotel was publisher Humphrey Thorpe-Fester. After the presentation, a lousy roast beef dinner was served, which should have been filet mignon, considering importance of the occasion.

We believe that in a Free Press, there is one side to every question

SOMETHING HILARIOUS HAPPENS ON THE CORNER OF MAIN AND THIRD

Something hilarious happened on the corner of Main and Third Streets last night. Every time we think about it, we laugh so hard we think we'll burst.

Originally, we had planned to report the details here. But now we've changed our minds. We're saving it so we can be the first to tell it at cocktail parties and social functions—before it gets around.

90

dependent in its attitude toward the public. And the way things look now, these "only" newspapers are going to be even more obnoxious, opinionated and independent than ever. In fact, if you live in a "one-newspaper town," you may be reading something like this in the very near future . . .

Monopoly

ause it's Festerville's **ONLY** Newspaper"

ther Report today because our Publisher is you're supposed to stay home and watch him.   WRITER: LARRY SIEGEL   PRICE: $1.50 PER COPY And we can get it, too!

OUR DYNAMIC PUBLISHER ADDRESSES MEETING OF TOWN CONSERVATIVES

Dynamic right-wing publisher Humphrey Thorpe-Fester spoke to leading town Conservatives at the Czar Nicholas Club on Elm St. last night. Subject of his talk was: "The Danger of Losing America to the Reds if Someone Starts Another Newspaper in this Town." Here you see, (right to extreme right) Mr. Thorpe-Fester; Amos Gorgg, founder of the "Kublai Khan Idealists"; Stanley Nobnock, Chairman, the "Louis XIV Dreamers"; and Sophie Ulster, Pres. of the "Daughters of the American Cavemen." Denied admission to lecture was Carl Pfrinz of the leftist "John Birch Society."

Brainy, Gorgeous Publisher's Wife Concludes Fabulously Absorbing Story

Selma Thorpe-Fester, the bright, witty, and lovely wife of publisher Humphrey Thorpe-Fester, informed *The Daily Monopoly* today that the dramatic and absorbing story of her appendicitis operation, which has been running daily in this paper in serial form for some time now, is finally over.

Charming Mrs. Selma Thorpe-Fester

Following is a run-down of some of the unimportant news stories which we were forced to omit to make room for Mrs. Thorpe-Fester's lengthy but fascinating account of her operation:

Sept. 2, 1945—World War II officially ended today when Japan surrendered aboard the battleship Missouri. Accepting their surrender on behalf of the victorious allies, Gen. Douglas MacArthur *(Cont. Pg. 13)*

EXCLUSIVE

Daily Monopoly Reporter Scores Big News Scoop

by Godfrey Zinn

In a town like Festerville, which has only one newspaper, it is naturally quite difficult to score a big news scoop on another paper. For that reason, we energetic, quick-thinking journalists on *The Daily Monopoly* have to do the next-best thing. We have to scoop each other!

I have information from a highly-reliable, unimpeachable source (namely our type-setter) that on Page 13 of today's paper there will be a poignant letter in the "Advice To The Lovelorn" column from somebody who calls herself "Worried." It seems that "Worried's" husband has been going out with another woman all along and when *(Cont. on page 12)*

MAYOR CALLS PRESS CONFERENCE

Mayor Fenwick Himp called a press conference in the Civic Auditorium yesterday to bring to the people the details of his new, highly-controversial City Traffic Control Plan, which this newspaper is against. Representatives of all the various newspapers in town are shown here: (left to right) Hollis Schnabble, of *The Daily Monopoly*. We won't bother you with details of the Mayor's ridiculous plan.

President Makes Ridiculous, Asinine, Idiotic Tax Suggestion To Congress

WASHINGTON, D.C., Feb. 14 — Miserable Democratic President John F. Kennedy, in a speech to a joint session of Congress yesterday, made one of the most insane tax suggestions in recent history. Honest to God, when we found out about it, we reporters who are writing this straight, unbiased news story got so sick to our stomachs we thought we'd die.

Do you know what this man who laughingly calls himself a "President" wants to do with *your money?*

Can you keep a straight face? He wants all entertainment expenses that are not directly connected with actual business procedures disallowed for deduction purposes on income tax reports. Now if that isn't a slap in the face to all American businessmen, and particularly to courageous, dynamic newspaper publishers with yachts and summer homes and chauffeur-driven Cadillacs to support, we don't know what is! Really, no kidding, do you think this is fair? We mean, how Communistic can you get?

Remember this: The Senate missed impeaching Andrew Johnson by just *one vote* in 1868. Let's make sure they don't miss *this time!* Write your Senator immediately! And make sure you send him a copy of this objective, un-biased, straight news story—together with the blistering Editorial on page 8, written by our courageous, dynamic newspaper publisher.

You may not agree with what we say, but you've got no choice

OVER THE YEARS with The Daily Monopoly

25 YEARS AGO TODAY: A brilliant, handsome, dynamic son was born today to *Daily Monopoly* publisher Humphrey Thorpe-Fester and his beautiful wife, Selma. The flawless child, named Henry, was delivered by Caesarian operation.

20 YEARS AGO TODAY: Publisher Humphrey Thorpe-Fester's brilliant five-year-old son, Henry, said his first word today: "Money!". He was also introduced to his mother for the first time. The latter had been away on a five-year tour of the Midwest, discussing her Caesarian operation.

15 YEARS AGO TODAY: Ten-year-old Henry Thorpe-Fester, gifted son of *Daily Monopoly* publisher, Humphrey Thorpe-Fester, was given a new lake today as a school promotion gift by his proud father. Tomorrow, Henry goes on to second grade. Congratulations, and lots of luck, Hank.

5 YEARS AGO TODAY: Twenty-year-old Henry Thorpe-Fester, publisher Humphrey Thorpe-Fester's brilliant and creative son, flunked out of Journalism School today for giving the five "W's" of news reporting as: Wine, Women, Welshing, Wasting, and Woolgathering.

TODAY: Twenty-five-year-old Henry Thorpe-Fester, talented son of publisher Humphrey Thorpe-Fester, today was turned down for a check at the Unemployment Bureau because of his inability to sign his name. He joins the staff of *The Daily Monopoly* tomorrow. Best of luck in your new job as Editor-In-Chief, Hank!

THE INQUIRING
PUBLISHER

QUESTION
Why are you so proud of me as a courageous dynamic publisher?
WHERE ASKED
Various places around my house.

Edna Thorpe-Fester
Loving Mother

Son, I'm proud of you for the same reason that any other average news-hungry citizen is proud of a newspaper publisher in an age of anxiety brought on by the threat of nuclear annihilation. First, because you always wear your muffler when it's cold outside. Second, because you drink your milk every day at 3 o'clock without me telling you to. Third, because you never holler on your children. And finally, because you make more money than a doctor even.

Horace Greeley Fester
Devoted Father

Gee, I don't know what to say! I mean, I'm so excited — to think — of all people in this whole wide house, you chose to interview me, a total father to you! Gosh-all-criminentlies. . . . Okay, enough of this humility garbage! You know damn well why I'm proud of you! You took a ridiculous, opinionated newspaper I founded 60 years ago, and kept it going as a family plaything. But if you ever change one Neanderthal policy, I'll break your courageous, dynamic neck!

Selma Thorpe-Fester
Loyal Wife

Humphrey, darling, I am proud of you because you have given me the opportunity to leave home and travel around the country for years on end, to bring to an eagerly awaiting nation the absorbing details of my various operations, despite the personal sacrifice and loneliness it meant to you.

Flora LaVie
Adoring Upstairs Maid

Humphrey, darling, I am proud of you because you have given your wife the opportunity to leave home and travel around the country for years on end, to bring to an eagerly awaiting nation the absorbing details of her various operations, so that you and I — what are you shushing me for?

94

LETTERS TO THE PUBLISHER

SHOCKED

Dear Sir:

I read your highly-opinionated, arch-conservative editorial of Feb. 10th, and was absolutely shocked by the terrible things you said about organized labor, medical care for the aged, Quentin Reynolds and Eleanor Roosevelt.

Westbrook Pegler,
New York City

NOTES

Dear Sir:

We realize that your newspaper is pretty much of a personal family thing with you, but may we make a small request? In the future, kindly leave notes to our milkmen in empty bottles outside your door at home, instead of publishing them on the editorial page of your paper. Sometimes, they are hard to find.

The Dairyfresh Milk Co.
Festerville

TIME CAPSULE

Dear Sir:

Thank you for offering to donate a copy of *The Daily Monopoly* for the new time capsule to be buried at the 1964 World's Fair in New York, to give future generations an idea of the quality of newspapers in one-newspaper towns. Unfortunately, we have already planned to include a copy of Pravda in the capsule, and we feel that your newspaper would be a duplication.

Robert Moses
New York City

CANDIDATE

Dear Sir:

Regarding your ultra-right-wing editorial of February 8th, we are pleased that you have expressed your desire to be a Republican candidate for office in 1964. However, we regret to inform you that, as of now, there are no plans for a contest for the office of "Emperor" in your state that year.

William F. Miller
Chairman, Republican Party
Washington, D.C.

PUZZLED

Dear Sir:

I realize that you don't give a damn about your readers, but there is such a thing as going too far. What I mean is, if you are going to run daily crossword puzzles, at least have the decency to use legitimate words. I have just seen the answer to your puzzle of Feb. 11, and I am positive that there is no such thing as a "Left-handed herniated Hopi Indian" called a "BVRTZ" or a "Southern Israel potato bug" called a "KRNXTL."

Margaret Farrar
New York City

95

BERG'S-EYE VIEW DEPT.

There's a big hullabaloo going on in this country about whether our young people are starting to date too early in life. Well, we don't mean to enter into this touchy controversy . . . but merely start another: Mainly, whether David Berg is starting to write about dating *too late* in life. You can all judge for yourselves as MAD presents

THE LIGHTER SIDE OF

DATING

WRITER & ARTIST: DAVID BERG

97

102

103

105

110

IN A MEN'S HABERDASHERY

MENS
HANDKERCHIEFS
5.00

ONE FALSE MOVE DEPT.

Basically, the game of chess is a game of "war." It was created many centuries ago, and so it was naturally based on war as it was waged in those times. The strategems employed, though classic, are completely anachronistic in the light of modern military science. That last sentence makes no sense to us whatsoever, but it does tend to lend a highly intellectual tone to an otherwise stupid article like this one is going to be. Anyway, let's just say that the kind of war the traditional chess game represents is a far cry from the kind of war nations would be moronic enough to fight today. And so, we propose that the game be brought up to date, that all pieces be re-designed, and that, while there's still time, we start playing MAD'S . . .

THE TRADITIONAL CHESS SET

Note how accurately this fine old antique chess set depicts the glory of ancient war. Note splendid royalty. Note bold knights. Note proud bishops. Note grand castles. Note haggard, tattered, hungry pawns who are in the front rows . . . and have to take most of the beating.

MODERN CHESS

ARTIST: BOB CLARKE WRITER: AL JAFFEE

MAD'S MODERN CHESS SET

Note how accurately this modern chess set depicts current cold war tactics. Note brilliant scientific pieces. Note terrified, neurotic pawns on brink of cracking up. Note one thing that hasn't changed. Pawns are still in front rows . . . and have to take most of the beating.

MOVES
The Old Way

Each traditional chess piece moves in a particular direction. This permits special intricate strategies that have fascinated brilliant minds for centuries. It also permits clods like us to come along with silly explanations of these intricate moves for clods like you.

PAWNS move ahead one square at a time except first move when two is optional. They move diagonally one square to capture opposing pieces.

KNIGHTS move in L-shape patterns in any direction — two squares ahead and one to the side (or is it one square ahead and two to the side?).

BISHOPS can move in any direction diagonally. A black bishop moves on black squares, and a red bishop is a terrible thing to call a bishop.

ROOKS (Castles) move in any direction in a straight line. Idea began when cheap ancient castle builders used to skimp on foundation mortar.

THE KING can make any kind of a move he might suddenly get an urge to make . . . but only one at a time. Game is over when King is captured.

THE QUEEN can make any move in any direction she wants to make in order to protect the King. His little game is over when she shows up.

PLAY
The Old Way

The exciting stimulation of ancient battle, realistically recreated on a game board with all of its clever strategies, has been thrilling the chess enthusiast for centuries. In the picture at the right, we see a typical spine-tingling competition. Note the wide-eyed concentration— Note the intense emotional strain— Note the anxious expectancy of the player on the right as he waits for the player on the left to make his move. Note that the player on the left has been dead for three years.

MOVES
The **NEW** Way

MAD's modern chess pieces are not limited to special moves. In fact, each move is completely unpredictable. Cunning, trickery, accident, sneakiness, surprise, fear, anxiety . . . any of these could play a vital part in the game. F'rinstance, a game might work like this —

Player on left blinks momentarily. Opponent quickly launches his ICBM Missile, attempting a sneak attack.

Player's early warning system, i.e. his Radar piece, picks up blips of opponent's approaching ICBM Missile.

Radar piece signals Air Raid Siren piece to sound alarm, and Fallout Shelter doors open automatically.

Pawns are then triggered to jump wildly into opened Fallout Shelters, but most are shot by first Pawn in.

Anti-Missile Missiles are launched automatically, thus automatically launching other offensive missiles.

Action continues until both sides' entire nuclear arsenal is launched — at which point, game is concluded.

PLAY
The **NEW** Way

MAD's Modern Chess Game is played pretty much as described above when it finally gets going. Strategy is limited to each player waiting for the other to make the first move. End of game is followed by deathly silence. Unlike old-fashioned chess, there is no winner. There is also no loser. After several years, the radiation subsides enough to permit another game to begin . . . if there's anyone left to play it. Also, a new chess set is used which MAD is now designing — with caveman-type pieces.

Antonio Prohias, who was forced to flee Cuba because he refused to become a "Castro Convertible", brings us another MAD installment of that friendly rivalry between the man in black and the man in white—better known as . . .

124

Here we go again with another primer. You all know what a Primer is. It's a simple book for the pupil who is just learning how to read. And so . . . for all those pupils who are just learning how to read, and are also graduating from High School this Spring, here is—

THE MAD College Primer

MY FIRST COLLEGE READER

Fresh Little Tales For Little Freshmen

Illustrated By Wally Wood   Written By Phil Hahn

LESSON 1.
The Professor

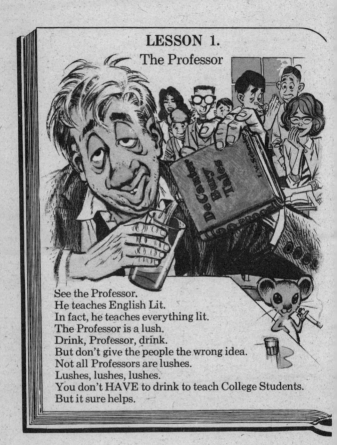

See the Professor.
He teaches English Lit.
In fact, he teaches everything lit.
The Professor is a lush.
Drink, Professor, drink.
But don't give the people the wrong idea.
Not all Professors are lushes.
Lushes, lushes, lushes.
You don't HAVE to drink to teach College Students.
But it sure helps.

LESSON 2.
The Co-ed

See the pretty Co-ed.
See the Co-ed's tight sweater.
See the Co-ed's tight skirt.
OK, better stop looking now.
Or else you'll scorch your eyeballs.
Scorch, eyeballs, scorch.
The Co-ed has an I.Q. of 67.
But she is an "A" student.
How can this be?
How, how, how?
Very simple.
Her instructors mark on the curve.

LESSON 3.
The Big-Man-On-Campus

See the Big-Man-On-Campus.
He is very important.
He is President of everything.
He belongs to 43 campus organizations.
Some of which don't even exist.
Join, B-M-O-C, join.
Soon you won't be Big anymore.
In fact, you won't even be On Campus.
You see, you forgot to enroll this term.
You were too busy going to meetings.

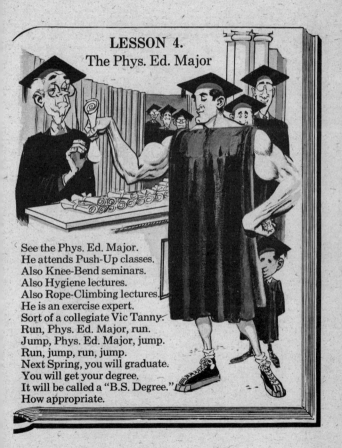

LESSON 4.
The Phys. Ed. Major

See the Phys. Ed. Major.
He attends Push-Up classes.
Also Knee-Bend seminars.
Also Hygiene lectures.
Also Rope-Climbing lectures.
He is an exercise expert.
Sort of a collegiate Vic Tanny.
Run, Phys. Ed. Major, run.
Jump, Phys. Ed. Major, jump.
Run, jump, run, jump.
Next Spring, you will graduate.
You will get your degree.
It will be called a "B.S. Degree."
How appropriate.

LESSON 5.
The Exchange Student

See the Exchange Student.
He is from Oxford.
He is here to learn about America.
Learn, Exchange Student, learn.
You will learn a lot in America.
You will learn to "Chug-a-lug."
You will learn to "Panty Raid."
You will learn to "Twist."
Do you know what else you will learn?
That you should have stayed at Oxford.

LESSON 6.
The Phony Intellectual

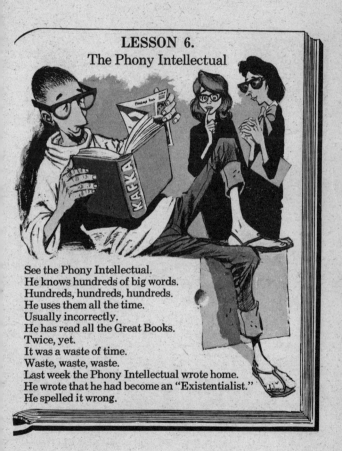

See the Phony Intellectual.
He knows hundreds of big words.
Hundreds, hundreds, hundreds.
He uses them all the time.
Usually incorrectly.
He has read all the Great Books.
Twice, yet.
It was a waste of time.
Waste, waste, waste.
Last week the Phony Intellectual wrote home.
He wrote that he had become an "Existentialist."
He spelled it wrong.

LESSON 7.
The Language Major

See the Language Major.
She loves Latin and Greek.
Also German, Gaelic and Sanskrit.
She is some kind of nut.
She speaks Middle English like Chaucer.
She speaks 14 Polynesian dialects.
Speak, speak, speak.
She can recite "Trees" in Swahili.
But nobody ever listens.
Languages are all she knows.
She is a crashing bore in 37 different languages.

LESSON 8.
The Cheerleaders

See the Cheerleaders.
They are full of energy.
They are full of enthusiasm.
Guess what else they are full of.
They yell "Go, team, go!"
"GO, TEAM, GO!"
Good heavens, what a racket.
Soon the crowd yells back:
"GO! GO! GO!"
But they don't mean the team.
They mean the Cheerleaders.
They want to watch the game in peace.

LESSON 9.
The Basketball Player

See the Basketball Player.
He loves to play Basketball.
He always has.
Always, always, always.
Ever since he was a little shaver.
Now he is a grown-up shaver.
He shaves points for gamblers.
Shave points, Basketball Player,
Shave points.
Soon the Law will be after you.
Soon you will have to make a break for it.
But fast.
In College Basketball
This is known as the "Fast Break."

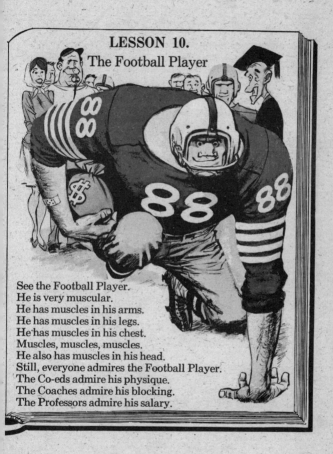

LESSON 10.
The Football Player

See the Football Player.
He is very muscular.
He has muscles in his arms.
He has muscles in his legs.
He has muscles in his chest.
Muscles, muscles, muscles.
He also has muscles in his head.
Still, everyone admires the Football Player.
The Co-eds admire his physique.
The Coaches admire his blocking.
The Professors admire his salary.

TODAY'S SER

ARE DATED AND

FOR EXAMPLE, LET'S EXAMINE TWO

The Caissons Go Rolling Along

Over hill, over dale,
We will hit the dusty trail,
As those caissons go rolling along.
Counter- march, right about,
Hear those wagon soldiers shout,
As those caissons go rolling along.

For it's "Hi-hi-hee!"
In the field artillery;
Shout out those numbers loud and strong:
(Three, Four)
And where 'er we go,
You will always know
That those caissons go rolling along.

In this age of military mobility, how many artillery men *march* over hill and dale . . . or anywhere else. And what's with this "wagon-soldier" bit? Sure, wagons were great during the Spanish American War (Teddy Roosevelt loved them!), but in today's army, they'd look ridiculous. And here's the thing that really gets us: Picture a bunch of tired, dirty, battle-sore soldiers slogging along after 2 weeks of combat—and then letting loose with something like "Hi-hi-hee!" Boy, that's not the kind of language they use in the army *we* know! Yep, this song has had it!

138

VICE SONGS

UNREALISTIC

OF THE MOST POPULAR ONES:

Anchors Aweigh!

Anchors aweigh, my boys!
Anchors aweigh!
Farewell to college days;
We sail at break of day-day-day-day!

Through our last night on shore,
Drink to the foam.
Un-til we meet once more,
Here's
Wishing you a
Hap-py voyage
Home!

This song was great for guys coming out of Annapolis. But you can't expect the *whole* Navy to keep singing it with enthusiasm. Let's face it: There are quite a few guys in the Navy who never even went to *high school,* let alone college. And another thing: Have you ever seen a bunch of sailors sitting around drinking? Can't you picture them toasting "the foam"? And saying something as clean and wholesome as, "Here's wishing you a happy voyage home!"? That's almost as bad as "Hi-hi-hee!" *This* song has had it!

OBVIOUSLY, IT'S TIME FOR A CHANGE,

SO HERE WE GO WITH...

MAD'S

REALISTIC,
UP-TO-DATE

SERVICE

SONGS

ARTIST: GEORGE WOODBRIDGE   WRITER: LARRY SIEGEL

With so many real soldiers playing extras in war movies, a song like this is appropriate:

THE CAMERAS GO ROLLING ALONG

(To the tune of "The Caissons Go Rolling Along")

Greet those fans, take a bow,
We're on movie duty now,
As those cameras go rolling along.
Hit the beach, kill a Hun
With those blanks there in your gun,
As those cameras go rolling along.

For it's "M-G-M"...
Or another "Warner's" gem...
To Dar-ryl F. Zanuck we belong:
(*Lights! Cut!*)
But should Reds attack,
We will all fight back...
Once those cameras stop rolling along.

Aside from heroism and devotion to duty, the Navy is famous for another thing: Dating horribly ugly girls. We think a song saluting this would be very apropos:

THE NAVY DATING SONG
(To the tune of "Anchors Aweigh!")

Our taste's absurd, my boys!
Our taste's absurd!
With girls, our eyesight's blurred:
We date pigs by the herd-herd-herd-herd!

When on that briny deep
From June to May,
Prac-tic'ly any creep
Looks
Like the girl
Who married JFK!

Here is a truly realistic "Marines' Hymn":

THE NEW MARINES' HYMN
(To the tune of the old "Marines' Hymn")

From the neck-high mud of fo-ox holes
To malar-i-a filled bogs,
We will march for 90 miles a day
And drop out and die like dogs!

We will land on mine-strewn bea-eaches
And we'll live with snakes and fleas;
Then we'll all leave Parris Island for
Restful combat overseas.

Since Federal troops have become part of the campus scenery at various schools over the past few years, we think it's time they were commemorated in song:

THE CAMPUS OCCUPATION SONG

(To the tune of "When Johnny Comes Marching Home")

When Johnny goes off to school again,
    Hurrah! Hurrah!
We Federal troops will be there then,
    Hurrah! Hurrah!
Oh, he'll sneer and jeer and scream and cuss,
And shout and yell and spit at us;
  What a hap-py day
When Johnny goes off to school.

When Johnny goes off to school once more,
    Hurrah! Hurrah!
We'll teach him the ways of total war,
    Hurrah! Hurrah!
He will learn his French and Arithmetic
To bayonets—not a hick'ry stick;
  And he'll whiff tear gas
When Johnny goes off to school.

When Johnny is through with school at last,
  Hurrah! Hurrah!
He'll leave the old campus and run off fast,
  Hurrah! Hurrah!
But then he'll be drafted and he'll come back
With helmet, gun and a full field pack,
  And they'll all curse HIM—
When Johnny comes back to school.

OL'BLOSSOM
UNIVERSITY

As we all know, astronauts have a problem more meaningful to them than space radiation and faulty rocket mechanisms:

THE MERCURY ASTRONAUT SONG
(To the tune of "The Air Force Song")

We can't zoom
High over land and waters;
We've no time
For the space scene,
Till we meet
Seventy-nine reporters,
Working for
Life Magazine.
(*Hold-That-Smile!*)
Cam'ras click;
They shoot our sons and daughters,
Dog and house;
Then they all roar:
"Make love to your wife
For page 8 of Life!"
Hey, nothing can stop the Henry Luce Corps!

One of the most common species of service life doesn't have his own song. This could be it:

THE GOLD BRICK SONG
(To the tune of "Bless 'Em All")

Bless Sick Call! Bless Sick Call!
When passion for duty is small,
We see the medics ere battles begin;
Tell 'em we're dying and need Aspirin.
How we Goldbricks just love that Sick Call;
It's safer than going A-WOL!
You get no promotion
With Calamine Lotion,
But who gives a damn—
Bless Sick Call!

And last but not least, this song needs no introduction:

SONG OF THE RESERVISTS
(CALLED BACK TO ACTIVE DUTY)

#$%&*!@¢!*&%$#!
#$%&*!@¢!
%$#!*&@¢!#%$¢%!
#$%&@&¢#!
%$#!
% #$!
#$%!
&@*¢$#*!#%$!
&@*#$%&*#@¢!
&$#%?#$&@#%!
#"/?¢&%$@ #*&%#"%&'*"!

G.WOODSBRIDGE

LOOK BEFORE YOU LEAP!

ARTIST: JOE ORLANDO
WRITER: SERGIO ARAGONES

A few issues back, you marvelled at the ingenious business
methods employed by "MAD'S Movie Theater Owner of the
Year." Well, those little tricks of his were "child's play"
compared to . . .

MAD'S

"DISCOUNT

CENTER"

OWNER

OF THE YEAR

WRITER: LARRY SIEGEL   ARTIST: WALLACE WOOD

Once again, **MAD** has assigned me to interview a prosperous business man, and get the inside story on his operation! Mr. **A.K. Kuttrayte,** owner of the nation's largest and most successful **Discount Center** . . . my name is **Dorothy Killfifth,** and I've been dying to meet you! You see, up to now, I thought **everybody** did all their shopping at **Tiffany's** . . . like **me!**

155

Now, I'll take you over to our "Garden Center" and explain our unique **pricing structure** here at "Kuttrayte City". It's only a short walk—about three or four miles . . .

What a hike! Am I glad I wore my Tiffany G.I.-Shoes today! Say, Mr. Kuttrayte, I notice that clock on the wall says 2:30! That's **wrong!** It's only **1:30** now . . . !

No, that clock is **right!** Our "Garden Center" is in **another time zone!**

Now, this power mower sells everywhere for about $64. So what **we** do is write down on the price tag: "**LIST PRICE: $112. OUR PRICE: —$64.!**" See, the trick is to make up a **ridiculous list price** for the tag and then sell the item for more or less what it **usually** sells for in the **first** place!

I see. In other words, the public only **thinks** they are saving money! But what happens when you put this same power mower on a "**Special Sale**"?

158

163

165

167

Well, Mr. Kuttrayte! I've seen enough! Enough to make me **sick!** Thank you!

Mr. Kuttrayte! Terrible news! P.U. Cuttpryce is opening a **new** Discount Center right across the street! He's calling it **"Cuttpryce County"**! And it's going to cover 1000 **more** acres than our store! His prices will be **lower,** he'll sell stuff we **don't** sell, and what's more—he's building an **apartment development** right in the store so people will never have to **leave** the place! What are we going to **do?**

DO? There's only one thing **to** do! Clear the store of people! Sheldon, get the oil-soaked rags! Herman, get the gasoline! Tony, get the blow torches! Frank, get the money from the safe! Sidney, get my insurance agent on the phone! I want to make sure I'm **covered** for the fire I'm about to have!

Everybody knows that record album covers are designed chiefly to sell the records inside. But, for a few discerning collectors, they also serve another purpose. Through the billings on the covers, it is possible to trace . . .

THE RISE...
...AND FALL

1948

1950

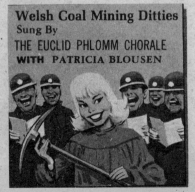

# of a
RECORDING
STAR

ARTIST: JACK RICKARD
WRITER: TOM KOCH

1952

Patricia Blousen
and the
EUCLID PHLOMM CHORALE
Sing
Tunes
That
Fell
Flat
On
Broadway

1954

1955

PATTI

1957

1959

1961

Patti Blousen
and the
Euclid Phlomm Chorale
Sing

SONGS OF
YESTERYEAR

1963

NAVAJO INDIAN RAIN CHANTS
WAILED BY
THE EUCLID PHLOMM CHORALE

The latest fad among boat owners is the use of pictorial yacht flags describing the various activities going on aboard. Like f'rinstance:

**Cocktail Party
In Progress**

**Wife Is
Ashore**

**Mother-In-Law
Is Aboard**

179

However, it seems to us that landlubbers could even make better use of these pennants. Here, then, is MAD's conception of pictorial —

YACHT FLAGS for the HOME

ARTIST: BOB CLARKE

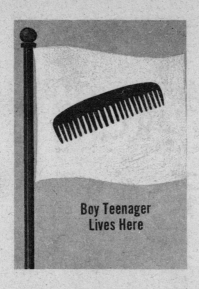

**Boy Teenager
Lives Here**

**Girl Teenager
Lives Here**

Father Of Teenager
Lives Here

College Basketball
Player Lives Here

"A" Student
Lives Here

"F" Student
Lives Here

Teenager Who Is
"Going Steady"
Lives Here

We're Having
Dinner At Home

We're Eating
Dinner Out

QU·2·5683

Teenager Who Would
Like To "Go Steady"
Lives Here

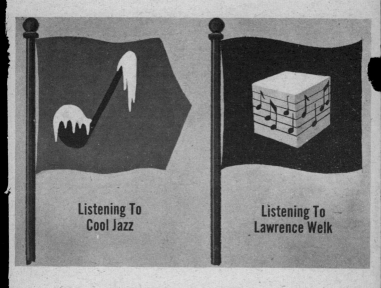

**Listening To
Cool Jazz**

**Listening To
Lawrence Welk**

Sunkist

**Used Car Dealer
Lives Here**

Disc Jockey
Lives Here

Golf Widow
Lives Here

N. Y. Met Fan
Lives Here

Do Not Disturb—
We're Watching TV!

TV Set On The Blink

(This flag is always
flown at half-mast)

We Have A
Fallout Shelter

Twist Party
In Progress

Family Fight
In Progress

THE INVENTOR
at the
NOVELTY COMPANY